YOUNG IKE

young Ike

· by Alden Hatch

illustrated by Jules Gotlieb

JULIAN MESSNER, Inc.   New York

Published by Julian Messner, Inc.
8 West 40th Street, New York 18

Published Simultaneously in Canada
by the Copp Clark Company, Ltd.

Copyright 1953 by Alden Hatch

Printed in the United States of America

Second Printing, November 1953

For

ALLENE

Acknowledgment

For the true stories of the early life of a very great American which are told in this book, I am indebted to many of the President's schoolmates in Abilene, to almost every member of his family, and particularly to Mrs. Eisenhower who has shown me unfailing kindness and has helped in every possible way.

Most of all I am grateful for the many long talks I have had with President Ike, from which I not only enriched my mind with his great knowledge of world affairs, but gained the inspiration which comes from personal contact with true nobility of mind and greatness of spirit.

Alden Hatch.

Somerleas
February 6, 1953

CONTENTS

CHAPTER 1

The House by the Railroad

"It's a fine fat baby boy," the doctor told David Eisenhower.

"Oh shucks!" said Ike's father. "We wanted a girl!"

The young Eisenhowers already had two boys, which was the reason for David's disappointment. But it was a lucky thing for America that the baby born to David Jacob and Ida Stover Eisenhower on October 14, 1890, in Denison, Texas, was a boy.

They named him David Dwight Eisenhower. Some twenty years later, when he went to West

Point, the Army got his names mixed up and arranged them the way they are known throughout the whole world—Dwight D. Eisenhower. His mother always called him Dwight. The story of how he was nicknamed Ike comes later.

The Eisenhowers were very poor at this time. Indeed, they never in all their lives had much money but that did not seem to make any difference to them. They lived in a small house made of unpainted clapboards, standing on stilts about a foot off the ground. On hot summer days when the temperature was over a hundred degrees, Ike's older brothers Arthur and Edgar liked to crawl into the cool darkness under the house and lie there peering out at the scorching white sunlight on the wide Texas prairie.

The house, which is still standing, looks funny and old fashioned now. It had three steep, pointed gables in front that stood up like a rabbit's ears—if a rabbit had three ears. There was a nice little porch where the older Eisenhowers used to sit in rocking chairs and look across the tawny fields that were so flat you could see the unbroken line of the horizon all around. Herds of goats grazed on the sun-parched grass. The Cotton Belt Railroad ran in front of the house. Bales of cotton were piled alongside the tracks waiting for the trains to come and take them to the big factories in the East to be made into

sheets and pillow cases, shirts and dresses. Ike's father, who was an engineer, ran a train on the railroad.

The most exciting thing in town was the twin ribbons of track. Gleaming, hissing steam engines pulled long, long trains of boxcars. They were loaded with cotton bales and the latticed cattle cars were packed full of bellowing Texas steers. Most fun of all was when the limited rolled to a stop with the big bell on the engine slowly clanging. The passengers from the East got out to stretch their legs on the open platform and stare at the little cluster of unpainted wooden houses that was Denison.

Life was not all fun and trains for Ike's brothers, however. Their parents believed that work was good for people. There was so much to be done around the house that the children were taught to be useful almost as soon as they could walk. When he was only four Arthur, who was a serious-minded little boy, was sent out to the vegetable garden to pick beans for the family dinner, and Edgar soon toddled after him. Ike missed both the trains and the bean picking, for he was less than two years old when the family moved back to Kansas.

Ida Stover Eisenhower, Ike's mother, was a plump young woman with masses of curly golden hair and vivid blue eyes. She radiated energy and never let the boys or her husband see when she was sad. She really ran the home, for Ike's father was a quiet, gentle man, who lacked his wife's strong character. Ida had gone to college, which was very unusual for a girl in those days.

No one ever knew how unhappy Ida was in Denison until one night when her husband came home with a letter clutched in his hand. He was unusually gay.

While she was kissing him "Hello," Ida caught a glimpse of the Kansas postmark on the envelope. "Who is it from, David?" she asked. "Is there good news?"

"The best ever," David answered. "It's from Father—and he says they are looking for an engineer to run the power plant of the Belle Springs Creamery in Abilene, Kansas. He thinks I might get the job."

"Abilene!" Ida cried, her eyes shooting blue sparks of excitement. "Oh, David, are we really going to live in Abilene?"

"Don't you like Denison?" David teased.

"Any place is good with you," Ida said stanchly. "But we've been so lonely here."

[5]

It was true. Both their families and all their friends lived in Kansas. David Eisenhower had owned a grocery store in Hope near Abilene. He was too vague and too kind hearted to be a good businessman, so he had lost all his money. Then he had taken a job on the Cotton Belt Railroad and moved to Denison. The Eisenhowers had lived there only a little over two years—not long enough to feel really at home.

"Are we really going to Kansas?" Ida asked again.

"I'm going to write Father this very evening," David assured her. "You'd better think about packing."

They started for Abilene on the train, with dozens of bags made of carpet cloth and all their furniture loaded in a boxcar. So before he was old enough to know it, Ike left his native state. But he never forgot that he had been born in Texas, that land of legendary heroes—like Sam Houston, who won its independence from Mexico; and Davy Crockett and Jim Bowie and the other brave men who died for freedom defending a little fort called the Alamo.

[6]

CHAPTER 2

Home in Abilene

The train stopped at the town of Chapman, Kansas, then started with a jerk of loose couplings. A conductor stuck his head in the door of the car and bellowed, "Next stop Abil-e-e-e-ne!"

Ike was standing on the red plush seat with his mother holding him by the skirt of his little dress; his turned-up nose was pressed firmly against the window. He had never seen so much green stuff. The fields were just as flat as Texas, but they were lush with long grass in which the cattle moved knee deep. Here and there the green was broken by a section of rippling, golden

[7]

wheat; in other places tall stalks of tasseled corn marched like soldiers toward the horizon.

The train jumped and bucked as the brakes went on, nearly throwing Ike off the seat. Ida began gathering up numerous bags and packages. Arthur and Edgar each had something to carry and Dad was burdened like a pack mule.

Uncle Abraham Lincoln Eisenhower stood on the Abilene station platform waving a greeting as the train came slowly in. Grandfather Jacob Eisenhower was there, too, dressed in his best black broadcloth suit for the great occasion. He had never seen his youngest grandson. Ike was not the least bit frightened and greeted his grandfather with a broad grin.

Dad looked across the tracks at a brick building as big as a carbarn, with a tall, thin smokestack that seemed about to poke through the sky. "Is that the new creamery?" he asked.

"Yes, David," said Grandfather Jacob. "It's got the finest stationary engine in central Kansas."

David's face was lighted by one of his rare smiles. "I can't wait to see it," he said, for he loved machinery. "Do you suppose I could take a peek at it before we go to the house?"

"No reason you shouldn't," Jacob answered. "You're going to be in charge of it from here on."

The Eisenhowers' first home in Abilene was a tiny cottage just south of the railroad tracks. It was much too small for them, especially after Ike's baby brother Roy was born. But after two or three years, Uncle Abraham went to California and the Eisenhowers moved into his house at 201 Fourth Street, where they lived for over half a century. Even after he grew up and got married and had houses of his own, Ike always thought of that little white house in Abilene as home. When he was far away in Europe, lonely for the people he loved and desperately tired from the responsibility of commanding a great army and the strain and danger and sadness of war, the thing he dreamed about was coming home to Abilene.

It was a pretty little house, almost exactly

square and made of white painted boards. The shingled roof looked like a pyramid with the point cut off. There was a chimney sticking up from its flat top.

Inside the house was the front parlor, a pleasant, sunny room with a bow window. It had shelves filled with books, for all the Eisenhowers loved to read. On a little table near the door was the family Bible, a massive ancient book printed in big clear type. It had wonderful pictures of Bible stories and brightly colored maps of the Holy Land. In the front was a blank page with lines on it, where Dad wrote the names of his children and the dates on which they were born.

Back of the parlor was a little room in which stood Mrs. Eisenhower's cherished upright piano. The boys liked to gather there and sing while their mother played hymns or the sweet old songs they all loved, like "Drink to Me Only with Thine Eyes," "Bells of St. Mary's" and "I Passed by Your Window."

The kitchen, where they spent most of their

time, was a long narrow room, with windows on both sides which made it very light and cheerful. The rest of the house consisted of small bedrooms. As two more boys were born, making six

brothers in all, they needed a lot of sleeping space.

When Ike was young there was no plumbing in the house. All the water had to be carried in from a well, and there was a little building out in back, called a privy, that served as a toilet.

There was plenty of land around the Eisenhowers' home—two and a half acres running up
to the railroad tracks on the north. On it they
raised almost all the food they needed—corn,
alfalfa, all kinds of garden vegetables and nearly
every possible kind of fruit tree. In addition,
they had pigs and Belgian hares—a large kind of
rabbit, very good to eat. The family also had a
team of horses and a cow. There was always at
least one dog.

Since Mr. Eisenhower worked at the creamery
all day, the boys had to do most of the chores on
the farm. The cow had to be milked, the horses
curried and fed; the hogs and chickens required
attention—and there were eggs to collect. In
the summertime they had to plow and plant,
weed the garden and hoe between the long, tall
rows of corn. It was hard work; but Ike can still
remember the wonderful fresh smell of the
fields in early morning and the cool feeling of
rich black earth between his bare toes. "It
seemed to send its goodness right up through
you," he once said, "as though you drew
strength from it like a plant."

Perhaps it really did have that effect, for all the Eisenhower boys grew up to be strong men.

The chore they all hated most, especially in winter, was getting up at half-past four in the morning to make a fire in the big kitchen coal stove. The boys took turns at this, each doing it for a week at a time. When it was Ike's turn somebody always had to wake him up—an alarm clock was no use at all. In fact he loved to sleep so much that it was almost as much trouble to get him out of bed as to go down and light the stove.

But the wonderful breakfasts that Ida cooked were worth all the trouble of getting the fire built. There would be crisp bacon from their own hogs, platters of fluffy scrambled eggs that had been laid that very morning, hot oatmeal with cream skimmed from the pail of milk the cow gave, and a heaping plate of biscuits.

The breakfast they all liked best was "mush and puddin'." The mush was fried corn meal which they grew and ground at home. Over it they poured the puddin', which was made of all the parts of a pig you did not usually eat—the

heart, liver and lights, bone marrow and strips of hide from which the bristles had been carefully scraped. It had to be cooked for hours until it was all melted down into a rich jellylike gravy that was so thick it was almost solid.

The only place you can get real honest-to-goodness puddin' is in central Kansas, and to this day General Ike will travel half across the country for a dish of mush and puddin'.

All the Eisenhower boys learned to cook. At their house Sunday was Mother's day off. In the morning, of course, they went to Sunday school and to church with their parents in the meeting-house the Brethren in Christ had built in Abilene.

After church the boys did all the housework and got a big Sunday dinner. The way they did it was more fun than work. Mother was banished completely from the kitchen—if she had seen them at work every hair on her head would have stood straight up.

All she ever knew was that her sons made wonderfully light piecrust. Their recipe was peculiar —to say the least. When the dough had been mixed in the usual way, the boys would roll it into a ball, then play a fast game of catch with it until it was thoroughly kneaded. If somebody missed a catch no one worried very much—the floor was always spotlessly clean.

Their method of washing dishes—when mother wasn't there—was equally spectacular. The boy at the sink would wash a dish and skim it across to the towel man who, after drying it, would complete the play to the stacker by the shelves. It was much more exciting than the pie game because a miss meant a broken plate; and too many broken plates meant a good sound spanking for somebody.

CHAPTER 3

"You'll Make a Fisherman Yet!"

The Eisenhowers had not always lived in Kansas.
Long ago Ike's ancestors came from the Palati-
nate of Bavaria, which is part of Germany. Their
name in German means iron striker.

Like the Pilgrims and the Puritans and many
other people, the Eisenhowers came to America
so they would be free to worship God in a way
they thought was right. They belonged to a re-
ligious group called the Brethren in Christ or,
sometimes, River Brethren because they used to
be baptized in rivers. The Brethren practiced a
strict but simple form of worship. Like the Quak-

ers, they did not believe in war or fighting of any kind.

In 1732 the Eisenhowers landed in America. They finally settled in Elizabethville, Pennsylvania. They soon had fine lands and a big brick house, which was also used for the meetings of the Brethren on Sundays. Ike's grandfather Jacob Frederick had a little cobbler's workshop in the attic where he repaired shoes for all the family.

About 1870 Grandfather Jacob decided to move to Kansas with many of the other Brethren. He sold his home and farm, loaded his family and furniture on a train and set off to start a new life in the West.

Young David Jacob, Ike's father, was sent to study engineering at Lane College at Lecompton, Kansas, which had just been founded by the Brethren. There he met Ike's mother.

Ida Stover came from Mount Sidney, Virginia. As a young girl she was a regular tomboy. Her greatest delight was to ride and hunt with her four brothers, who teased her for being a girl, but adored her.

"YOU'LL MAKE A FISHERMAN YET!"

When their parents died the Stover boys went west to make their fortunes. Ida remained with an uncle and aunt in Virginia until she was twenty-one. Then she set out alone for Kansas to join her beloved brothers.

If she had stayed in Virginia she might never have gone to college; but in the West everything was new and stimulating. To the pioneers, education was the greatest boon of all; women as well as men sought it eagerly. Ida decided to use her small inheritance to educate herself. At college she studied history, English and music—and to her, the greatest of these was music. She used the last of her money to buy the little upright piano which Ike remembers so happily.

David Eisenhower and Ida Stover were married at Lane College on September 23, 1885. Their wedding certificate hangs above the family Bible in the house in Abilene. Besides the beautifully engraved writing on it, there are three photographs. The picture of the groom shows a slim young man with straight, dark hair and intense brown eyes. Facing him, his bride looks so alive that she fairly seems to leap out of the faded picture. The third photograph is that of the minister who married them.

When Ike was seven years old he started school in a small wooden schoolhouse only about a block from where he lived. He was a solidly built little fellow, with yellow hair and bright blue eyes, very active and scrappy. He was forever getting into trouble, but his wonderful, lopsided grin usually got him out of it.

That first day in school the children crowded around the new kid at recess, asking, "What's your name?"

"Dwight Eisenhower," he answered.

"Let's call him Ike," somebody yelled.

"We've already got an Ike Eisenhower," one boy objected, for Ike's older brother Edgar was called Ike.

"Edgar can be Big Ike and this one Little Ike," announced a big eighth grader.

That decided it. The children seemed to feel that Ike was a good name to go with Eisenhower. Later at the same school the younger Eisenhower boys, Roy and Earl, were known as Big Ike and

Little Ike. When they left school the other brothers were again called by their right names; but for some unknown reason the General was always called Ike.

Dad and Mother Eisenhower never did get that girl they wanted so badly. Their sixth son, Ike's favorite brother Milton, was born in 1899. His parents were so disappointed that they pretended he was a girl, making him wear his hair in long corkscrew curls until he was nearly five years old. It was pretty rough on Milton.

Despite his curls, Milton was no sissy—in fact they made him the scrappiest of the family. Being the youngest, he had to work very hard to keep up with his strenuous brothers.

Baseball was their favorite game. They had a diamond out back of the house. The privy behind home plate made an excellent backstop. In summer they went swimming in aptly named Mud Creek, or the clear cold waters of the Smoky Hill River.

Kansas gets very hot in summer, but it is equally cold in winter. When the river froze, Ike and the other Abilene boys used to play hockey on it with crooked branches for sticks and an old tin can for a puck. Sometimes there would be ten or twelve boys on a side. They would fall all over each other on the narrow, twisting surface of the ice. While it was not a bit like the hockey played by crack school and college teams, it was a lot more fun.

The river was good for fishing, too. Even before Ike started school he learned to fish. One day as Arthur and Edgar were planning to go angling, Ike said, "Can't I go, too?"

"You'll be in the way," Arthur objected. "You'll make a noise and scare the fish."

"I know better than that," Ike said stoutly.

"Let him come," Edgar put in. "I'll cut him a pole while he digs worms."

The spade they had was bigger than Ike, so it ended with Arthur digging while his little brother pulled the worms out of the newly turned earth and popped them into an old tin can.

"YOU'LL MAKE A FISHERMAN YET!"

Ike felt very manly as he trudged across the fields carrying the new pole. When they got to the river Edgar showed him how to bait the hook.

"Now you watch that piece of cork on your line," he told Ike. "If it takes a sudden dive, give it a quick jerk."

He went off a little way with Arthur. Ike sat very still for what seemed hours—it was really about three minutes. Then the cork wobbled slightly and he gave a tremendous jerk. Out came the hook; off flew the worm. There was no fish.

"I've lost my worm," he yelled appealingly to his brothers.

"Bait it yourself—and shut up!"

Somehow Ike managed to get a slippery worm speared on the hook. This time he sat even more quietly than before—so still that he almost went to sleep in the hot sun. Suddenly the cork went right under. Ike gave a convulsive jerk and his pole bent double. Whatever was on the other end jerked right back.

"I've got a whale!" he yelled.

Arthur and Edgar came running. Ike danced around trying to pull in his fish. His brothers were jumping up and down yelling advice. It was the most exciting moment Ike had ever known.

The fish got tired before he did, and Ike dragged it flopping up onto the muddy shore. It had a ferocious-looking face with long whiskers.

"What is it, a shark?" he asked, awed by his own prowess.

"Just a catfish," said Arthur.

"But a big one," Edgar added. "You'll make a fisherman yet, Ike!"

CHAPTER 4

Castaways

The Smoky Hill River was not always gentle and friendly. One rainy spring it swelled to a great boiling torrent that roared along, gouging its banks until huge pieces of earth caved in and were churned to froth by the flood. Finally the banks were not high enough to hold it in. The water poured over them and spread slowly across the level plain like chocolate sauce over a brick of ice cream.

The brown water seeped through the streets of Abilene, which at that time had wooden sidewalks on stilts about two feet high. It came al-

[25]

most to the top of these walks and spread over the railroad tracks and around the Eisenhowers' house, flooding the cellar. Ike and Edgar took off their shoes and stockings and went splashing around through the icy water, which was over a foot deep. It was great fun.

Older people did not agree about that. They hated to have to wade home from work. The man who lived in the house across Fourth Street had a better idea. He borrowed a skiff and came rowing right up the middle of the road. Hitching his boat to the porch rail he picked up the oars and went into his house.

Edgar and Ike eyed the skiff longingly. They loved a boat ride on the river—and how much more exciting it would be to sail right through town!

"Let's go across and look her over," Ike suggested.

"All right," agreed Edgar.

They splashed across the street. The boat rocked gently, on the little waves they made. Of course they climbed aboard.

For a few minutes they pretended they were

sailing along. Then Edgar began to fiddle with the rope that held the boat to the house. "Do you dare me to untie it?" he asked hopefully.

Ike obliged. "Sure I dare you!"

Edgar clumsily untied the knot and gave a little push. The boat moved backward and then began to drift slowly along between the houses and trees in the general direction of the river. The boys had no oars or any way of steering, but that did not worry them. Sailing over the prairie was very exhilarating.

Some farmers, who were putting their horses up for the night, happened to see a rowboat drifting across the plain. It was heading straight for destruction in the roaring, tumbling violence of the river itself. To their horror, the men spied two small boys standing up in the little craft. They seemed to be waving their arms and screaming for help.

The boat was going much faster now; the men

knew they didn't have a chance to catch it on foot. So they mounted their big farm horses bareback and went galloping across the watery fields. The horses splashed and slipped, but they were catching up with the boat.

As they got closer, one of the men shouted, "Those fool kids ain't hollerin' for help. They're singing!"

Soon they could all hear the words of the song:

*And so we sang the chorus from Atlanta to
    the sea,
While we were marching through Georgia.*

Just before it reached the main part of the river, the bottom of the boat hit a hummock of land and stopped short, throwing the boys off their feet. The men came galloping up and jumped off their horses thigh deep in water. They yanked the boys roughly out of the boat and set them on the panting horses. One of the men tied the rope around his waist and towed the skiff back.

Ike could not see why they were all so angry. It had been a lovely sail.

The other time young Ike came close to death it was not his fault at all. One day when he was about twelve years old he fell in the stable yard and scratched his knee. It was not much of a cut so he paid it no mind. But stables are very risky places to play in, because of the dirt from the animals.

Two days later Ike's leg was badly swollen, but he went to school anyhow. When he got home that night his leg throbbed and burned. His foot was so swollen that his parents had to cut his shoe off. The doctor came to examine his leg. When he touched it very gently, Ike almost screamed with pain.

The doctor looked frighteningly grim. "Blood poisoning!" he said.

Those were dreadful words in that far-off time. Nowadays the wonderful new drugs that scientists have discovered will cure such an infection in no time; then, however, you might easily die from it.

When the doctor came next morning Ike was worse. The lower part of his leg had turned black and the thigh had swollen until it was as big as his body.

"We've got to amputate," the doctor told Ike's mother.

Ida turned white and her lips moved in prayer.

"Do you mean cut it off?" Ike asked.

"Yes, son," the doctor said sadly. "It's the only chance of saving your life."

"No!" Ike said violently. "I'd rather die."

Ida Eisenhower was a woman with an unusual sort of courage—the strength of character to let her children make their own decisions. Though the doctor pleaded with her to agree to the operation, she would not let him do it since Ike refused.

The boy seemed to get worse every hour. His temperature was way above a hundred and the pain throbbed and burned all through his body. He asked for a fork and sat up in bed, chipping at his teeth with it. In some strange way it seemed to help him bear the agony of his fiery leg.

On the third day Ike got really frightened. His high temperature made his mind hazy; hours passed when he remembered nothing. He had heard about people getting delirious, and he knew that was happening to him. He thought he was going to die, but his spirit was stronger than his physical power.

"Edgar," he shouted, "Edgar!"

His older brother came in with the sad, embarrassed look that people get when they know you are very sick.

"What can I do for you, Ike?" he asked.

"Look, Edgar, you got to promise me something," Ike said tensely.

"Sure, I'll promise. Anything!"

"I'm going off my nut, Edgar. It comes in

waves—and it's getting worse. You've got to stay here on guard so they won't cut off my leg when I'm unconscious. Promise you won't leave me even for a second. Promise you won't let them!"

Solemnly Edgar said, "I promise."

All through the dreadful days and nights that followed, Edgar kept his word. By day he sat on a little chair beside Ike's bed. He would not even go downstairs to eat, so Ida brought his meals up to him. At night Edgar slept on the floor in front of his brother's door.

The doctor came and pleaded to be allowed to save Ike's life. He got angry and talked about it being murder. Finally one night he said, "Even amputation will not save him now. Only a miracle can."

Ida and David prayed all that night. The boys prayed, too, even little Milton.

In the morning Ike was better. His temperature slowly dropped, while the swelling began to go down. The miracle had happened.

Three weeks later Ike was walking around. His leg was as good as ever—strong enough to carry a soldier into battle.

CHAPTER 5

The Closed Ring

When Ike was entering his teens the Eisenhowers' family life reached its peak of jollity and comradeship. All the boys were home, for Arthur had not yet gone off to Kansas City to start his business life, and Milton, who was nine years younger than Ike, had developed from a baby into a boy, though he still wore those hateful curls!

It was then that the family bonds were so closely woven by work and happiness and troubles shared that they remained the strongest tie in the lives of all the brothers. After they were all grown up and scattered to the far ends of the country, their greatest joy was to get together in a rousing family reunion.

How the little house on Fourth Street must have shaken to the thundering feet of boys dashing up and down the stairs all day long—heavily booted feet in winter, bare feet in summer. For the brothers enjoyed that almost forgotten freedom of the American boy to go shoeless from June to September, thereby saving a lot of shoe leather.

The wonderful meals in the long, sunny kitchen were as raucous as a convention of Kilkenny cats. Every one of the boys had strong opinions and voiced them at the tops of their lungs.

Even noisier were the evenings when they gathered around the little upright piano. Ida valiantly thumped out their favorite melodies, trying to hold them to the tune, while seven voices—ranging from her husband's deep baritone to Milton's shrill treble—sang as loudly as they could in anything but close harmony.

Not that it was all sweetness and light at the Eisenhowers'. The boys were very different individuals who clashed continuously.

Arthur was the most serious. He was already doing a man's work at the creamery and accepting a man's responsibility. Edgar was big for his age, determined to have his own way. Ike was carefree and independent—taking none of Edgar's lip without a fight.

Among the younger boys, Roy was more nearly like Arthur—rather sober, though less efficient. Earl was at this time just a kid who tried to imitate his bigger brothers, except that even then he showed more of his father's mechanical ability than any of the others.

As for Milton, it was a great mistake to be misled by the angelic, dreamy look of his face, framed in those memorable ringlets. Milton would fight anybody at the drop of a hat, and they did not have to drop it far.

For some reason Milton and Ike were the closest of the brothers. Perhaps it was because the nine years' difference in their ages was just right so that Ike felt protective without being condescending, while Milton could look up to him without feeling that he belonged to the remote world of grownups. Or possibly it was because their temperaments and minds were so

much alike that when they both grew up they knew without talking about it just what each would think about any given thing.

On the other hand, Ike and Edgar were continually fighting. Edgar always won. He was a year and a half older and he also grew faster.

Though Ike got licked every time, that did not stop him—nor would Ida interfere.

One time they had a terrific battle in the kitchen while Ida was cooking dinner. Howls and yells of pain brought Earl rushing in from play. He saw his mother placidly working at the stove, while almost under her feet Edgar was sitting on top of Ike, banging his yellow head against the floor.

"Give up?" growled Edgar.

"No! Ooww!"

"Say Uncle!"

"No! Help! You beast!"

It was more than Earl could take. He flew at Edgar with all his puny might. Ida turned calmly around and scooped him off.

"Let them settle it," she said. "If anybody interferes they'll just stay mad at each other. This way they'll be friends again in five minutes."

And they were.

For years Ike dreamed of getting big enough to beat Edgar. Finally, when he had established himself as a crack heavyweight boxer at West

Point, he wrote to Edgar. "How about a little fight next time we meet?"

Edgar, who was no fool, wrote back: "Sure— with cream puffs at twenty paces."

When they were not fighting, Ike and Edgar were aiding, abetting and daring each other into all sorts of scrapes like their wild ride in the rowboat. All the boys used to play tag around the barn, in and out of the hayloft and along its steeply sloping roof. But only Edgar and Ike, daring each other on, ever climbed up on top of the veterinary's sign that their uncle had erected on its very pinnacle. Of course they got whipped by Ida, whose hands-off policy did not go as far as letting them frighten her half to death. And of course they soon did it again.

When there was work to be done, which was a good deal of the time, all the brothers co-operated. And despite the warfare which raged within the family, they stood together against the rest of the world.

"We were a closed ring," Ike says.

So they were. Father, Mother, and the six boys

all thought of themselves as one unit. Anything might happen within the ring—and that was no outsider's business. They all made forays outside it, for fun or study or to make money. They each had their own good friends to whom they were as devoted as pals can be. But those things belonged outside.

The family was like a fortress in which they were safe and warmly happy. It gave them all a wonderful sense of being secure. They always knew that all the Eisenhowers would rally around when any one of them was hurt or in trouble—that home meant a place where you loved everyone and everyone loved you.

CHAPTER 6

Learning History

General Ike thinks that the most important thing of all to learn is history. If you know history you have the benefit of the wisdom and experience and courage with which great men of all nations have solved the problems of their time. You can also profit by the mistakes which people made long ago, and draw inspiration from the ideals of those who led the way to better things.

Ike's intense interest in history began when he was about thirteen. It began at home.

Abilene is a very historic town. In the old days before the railroad was completed to Texas, the tracks did not run beyond this point—it was called "The End of Steel." The Texans, who raised a lot of cattle to feed the people in the East, had to drive them in great herds nearly a thousand miles across the prairie. The route they followed was called the Chisholm Trail.

Abilene was the head of the Chisholm Trail. When the longhorn steers got there, they were loaded onto trains and sent to all the cities of the East. Sometimes there would be a hundred thousand head of cattle in great pens outside of town waiting their turn to be loaded.

At such times Abilene was crowded with cowboys. They were a rootin', tootin' gang of reckless young men who were out for a good time. They were very quick on the draw. To stop the gun fighting, the town hired famous Wild Bill Hickok to be marshal and keep the peace. Wild Bill was quicker with a gun and a better shot than anyone else. He made Abilene law abiding.

When the rails were pushed on across the plains to Texas, Abilene settled back to be the sleepy little town where Ike grew up. But he loved to read the stories about the cowboys and look at the very houses where some of the famous gun fights had taken place.

From reading about his own town, Ike went on to read all the history books he could lay hands on, and so, without realizing it, he fitted himself for his great role in *making* history.

Ike began going to high school in a firehouse. It was also the city hall—and the biggest and fanciest building in Abilene. It was made of dark red brick with many bulges and bays and bastions. There were stone arches over the doors and windows. The elaborate structure was topped by a bell tower that looked like a brick beehive.

The ground floor was divided into two big rooms. The hand-drawn pumper of the Volunteer Fire Department was kept in one room. The other doubled as the council chamber and a one-room school, where the boys and girls of all the high school classes studied together. The rope from the big iron bell in the tower hung down through a hole in the ceiling.

On a day in early fall, soon after Ike started high school, he was studying his grammar. It was a sleepy sort of day with the warmth of summer still heavy in the air and big bluebottle flies buzzing against the windowpanes. The Senior Class droned through its geography lesson. Everybody, including the teacher, was drowsy.

Bang! The heavy oak door crashed open and a wild-eyed man rushed into the room.

"Fire!" he shouted. "Jim Royer's barn's afire!"

He sprang at the bell rope and swung on it. Overhead the iron bell clanged out the alarm. Its vibrations singing through the building, seemed to come up from the floors through the soles of the feet.

Everybody jumped up shouting. There was a wild stampede for the hose cart. Men were pouring out of shops and offices all along Broadway. The Volunteers came running with rubber coats streaming behind them, helmets clutched to their heads.

They formed up on the drag ropes of the engine. Their captain bellowed through his speaking trumpet, "Come on, boys!" And off they went, with the engine jumping and slewing behind. The crowd raced along with them. Dogs barked, horses shied. The entire Abilene High

School—boys, girls and teacher—tore along in their wake.

It was a splendid fire. Nobody got hurt. The Volunteers were brave and skillful. And Ike, together with most of his schoolmates, had a wonderful time taking turns on the seesaw hand pumps of the engine, getting thoroughly soaked by the hose and dirty from smoke and soot.

When Abilene High was moved into its own fine new building on the edge of town two years later, going to school was not nearly so much fun.

All the Eisenhower boys worked at part-time jobs to bring a little extra money into the family till. Long before he went to high school, when he was no more than eight or nine years old, Ike and his brother Edgar used to fill their little express wagon with fresh vegetables they had grown, and peddle them at the back doors of the houses north of the tracks where the wealthier families of Abilene lived.

There were lots of other jobs open to Abilene boys, such as mowing lawns and delivering the two rival papers, the Abilene *Reflector* and the Abilene *Chronicle*. There were odd jobs at the Abilene Bottling Company and work sandpapering the wooden animals in the merry-go-round factory. In summer they helped harvest wheat and corn. At one time or another, Ike worked at most of these things.

In 1905, when he was eighteen years old, Arthur went to Kansas City to make his own way in the world. In order to get a good early start job hunting in the big city, he got up in the middle of the night and took the 4:00 A.M. train. He had two twenty-dollar gold pieces in his pocket.

The station at Kansas City is down under a high bluff. Arthur found a row of one-horse cabs waiting there and asked one of the cabbies, "How much to take me to a boardinghouse on top of the hill?"

"Fifty cents."

Arthur shook his head—that was a huge amount of money to him. He went down the line of cabs and tried the last one. The price was still fifty cents.

As the boy hesitated, a kind-seeming man asked him what the trouble was. Arthur explained that fifty cents was too much for a cab ride.

"Follow me," said the man, and led the way through an alley to where a spring wagon stood waiting.

Arthur put his suitcase in the back and climbed up on the seat with his new friend, who drove him up the steep hill and stopped in front of a boardinghouse.

"Thank you ever so much," Arthur said. "What do I owe you?"

"That will be fifty cents," was the answer.

As soon as he had left his bag, Arthur started looking for work. His method was to walk down Tenth Street stopping in every place of business to ask for a job. When he got to the Commerce Trust Company he was hired as a messenger boy at twenty-five dollars a month.

Arthur never has changed his business. He is now executive vice president of the Commerce Trust Company, which means that he runs the biggest bank in Kansas City.

With Arthur gone, Edgar and Ike really had

to get down to work to supplement the family income. That summer Ike got a job in the creamery. In the hot months selling ice was one of the biggest deals at the creamery. It was made in the freezing room, the floor of which was a checkerboard of small trap floors, each with a brass ring. When a door was raised there was a cake of ice in a steel tray, very much like the ice cubes in a modern refrigerator—only those ice cubes each weighed three hundred pounds.

The ice trays rested in brine, which was kept at twenty degrees. When the ice had frozen good and solid, Ike, who had grown very strong, would run a small crane up to one of the trays, hitch the chain to a crossbar and haul it out by turning a big crank that worked the gears. In the ice storage room the cakes were tipped out of the trays and stacked up by hand.

In July and August the thermometer often goes over one hundred in Abilene. Working in such heat, Ike dripped perspiration. When he went to the ice storage room the breath of winter hit him like a blow. The sweat froze on his body and his shirt crackled with thin ice. It would have been easy to catch pneumonia, but he was in such good condition that he never did.

Milton and Earl liked to walk over and watch Ike loading the ice wagons. He looked tremen-

dously strong to them as he lifted a hundred-pound piece of ice in his tongs and swung it over the tail of the truck. Of course when they were watching he worked with an extra flourish to show off.

LEARNING HISTORY

When September came, Ike had to go back to school, but he also had to keep on earning money. So he and Edgar took a job between them —the position of night fireman at the creamery.

They worked alternately. One night Ike would sleep while Edgar worked. The next time it would be Ike's turn to sit up all night.

The engine room was enormously high. On one side of it was the stationary steam engine, with its big flywheel and darkly shining connecting rods, its fat, upright cylinders and rows of gauges. Its iron supporting columns were painted a brilliant red with BELLE SPRINGS CREAMERY in gold letters across them.

Beyond the engine were the huge silver boilers with numerous fire doors in their lower faces. Ike's job was to keep the fires going—and just enough steam in the boilers so they would be ready to start up when his father arrived in the morning.

He had a tattered easy chair in the middle of the room. There he studied his homework by the light of an unshaded bulb which hung on a long cord from the ceiling. Sometimes he simply snoozed, waking every hour to read the gauges in the boilers and shovel coal into the fires.

Though it seems odd, that, too, was part of his training to be a soldier. The ability to sleep in snatches for a few minutes at a time is important under the strain of war. Many famous generals—among them Napoleon and General Jeb Stuart—had this useful trick. Ike learned it during the long winter nights in the engine room of the Belle Springs Creamery.

CHAPTER 7

The Bums of Lawzy Loo

Though Ike worked very hard, he had such tremendous energy that he was never too tired for fun. There were lots of nice young people in the class of 1909 at high school—most of them still live in Abilene. His best friends among the boys were Bruce Hurd, Charlie Chase, the Sterl boys, Harry Makin, Herb Sommers, and Paul Royer. Then there was John MacDonell, who was nicknamed Six. Although he was two years younger than Ike, he became his closest friend.

Ike liked the girls, too, especially Ceil Curry, who lived in the next block. She was a slim, pretty girl with straight features and brilliant hazel eyes. Her light brown hair was drawn smoothly back to a Grecian knot. Ceil and Ike often walked home from school together. He gallantly carried her books.

The boys and girls of Ike's crowd had a sort of club. For some reason that nobody can remember, they called themselves "The Bums of Lawzy Loo."

The Bums had a very good time in the pleasant, informal ways of a small town in the 1900's. They often picnicked on the river where they had a shack which they called Camp Noise. There were no movies in those days and nobody owned an automobile, so in the evenings they went for walks or met at somebody's house to play parlor games and ask riddles. Sometimes they danced to the music of a phonograph, which had recently been invented.

Ike loved to sing, which was one thing he did *not* do well. When he felt really good, he lifted his powerful voice in "Daisy, Daisy, Tell Me Your Answer True. . . ."

Though he knew all the words, he was not

within shouting distance of the right key, and before he was halfway through his friends would roar in anguish, "For the love of Mike, SHUT UP!"

At high school Ike's favorite game was football. After a summer of manhandling ice at the creamery, his muscles were as hard as steel wire. He was big and tough, though a little slow. They made him tackle on the varsity team. (Later when he developed speed as well as brawn, he played halfback.)

In Ike's Senior year there was a serious crisis at Abilene High. The authorities decided that the school must economize. They chose to do it in what the boys considered the worst possible way, by cutting down on athletics. The announcement went out: "There will be no football coach this year. Expenses for out-of-town games cannot be paid by the school."

As they read the notice the team was filled with black despair. There was an indignation meeting on the desolate gridiron and everyone raged. You could not print the things they called the school board. But that did not help.

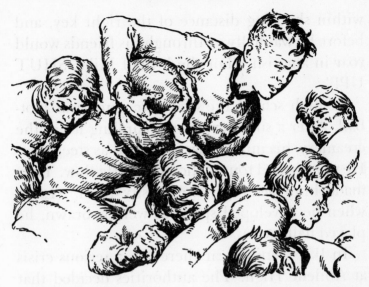

Ike was the only one who had a constructive idea. "Let's form an athletic association and raise the money."

"Who, us?" asked Six MacDonell.

"Why not? We ain't hogbound, tied or chained."

Wild enthusiasm succeeded despair. Everybody talked at once. Fantastic plans for raising money were mooted and booted around.

"One thing's sure, Ike's got to be president," said Harry Makin.

"Why not Six?" Ike asked.

"No," said Six. "It's your idea, and you got to put it across. Ike for president!"

"Aye!" It was a solid shout.

So Ike became the first president of the Abilene High School Athletic Association. Though most of the joyous schemes of high finance never got beyond the dreaming stage, the association saved football at Abilene. It is still functioning today.

The first crisis came the week before the team was supposed to go to Chapman for the annual game with that high school. There was absolutely no money in the till, and Chapman was twelve long, long miles to the east up the Union Pacific tracks. You could not hitch a ride either, for there was virtually no automobile traffic.

"You're the president of the association," his teammates told Ike. "Do something!"

"All trains ain't passenger trains," Ike observed, looking wise. "And all the people who ride on them ain't exactly passengers."

The boys got the idea. When the eleven-thirty freight (eastbound) groaned onto the siding to let the Denver-Kansas City Limited through, eleven football players and two substitutes were hanging around trying to look nonchalant. The Limited thundered past on time and a brakeman threw the siding switch. The freight engine snorted twice slowly, then six times fast as the drivers spun. Couplings banged, wheels groaned and the long line of freight cars inched forward while the train crew swung aboard.

"Now!" Ike shouted.

Thirteen boys dove under the slowly moving train and scrambled onto the tie rods which braced the bottoms of the boxcars.

Ike found himself lying on his stomach with his nose pressed between the steel rods—barely two feet above the cinder roadbed. He was getting a worm's-eye view of the world.

As the train moved onto the main line and gathered speed, suction lifted dust and cinders off the ties in a choking cloud. Ike's eyes were full of grit and he could hardly breathe. He grasped the rods with the deadly grip of panic and rode blindly on. The scream of wheels on rails, the rattle and bang of loose parts and the roar of speed-created wind deafened him.

After what seemed ages of misery came a series of racking jolts as the brakes went on. The train slowed and stopped. Out from under the cars rolled the football heroes of Abilene. Their faces were so covered with coal dust that they looked like an old-fashioned minstrel troupe.

But it was worth it! They beat Chapman High —and their homeward trip on the rods of the No. 6 mixed freight did not seem nearly as tough.

Probably the peak of Ike's football career in high school came nearly two years after he was graduated. He was back in school studying for his entrance examinations to West Point. There were no formal rules about who could play football, so he went on the team again.

That year they played the high school at Salina, Kansas. It was a much larger school than Abilene—and with all that material to draw from, it naturally had a better team. Abilene's only chance was for its stars Ike and Six MacDonell to play every minute of the game. They had to carry the rest of the team on their shoulders.

Salina had a delayed line plunge that was very successful. Ike figured the play early in the game, and after that his one hundred and seventy pounds of work-hardened muscle smashed it every time.

"Who is that big Swede?" Salina's coach asked, eying Ike's yellow hair and ruddy face. "We'd like to have a player like him."

The Salina boys were not as complimentary as their coach. They got mad at having their best plays smashed by one man. Nobody wanted to tangle with "the big Swede," so they picked on Six who was as fast as lightning, but very light. Four of Salina's linesmen jumped him in a mass play. When the scrambled mess of arms and legs and bodies was pried apart poor Six lay unconscious on the turf.

At the sight of his friend's limp form, Ike went into action. He hated foul play and this was the worst yet.

A flaming yellow fury hit the Salina team. For a moment or two nobody quite knew what was happening. But when it was over, the four Salina linesmen were stretched peacefully on the ground beside their unconscious victim.

Ike played other games besides football. In the spring he and MacDonell starred on the baseball team. Six, a southpaw, was best at this and captain of the team. They both dreamed of someday playing in the far-off, fabulous major leagues.

Since there was no gymnasium at Abilene High, sports were out during the winter. Their place was taken by rehearsals for the school play. In Ike's Senior year it was the *Merchant of Venice,* and Ike played the part of Launcelot Gobbo. According to those who saw it, his performance was no great addition to the drama. The truth is that Ike was never able to pretend emotions he did not feel. He was too *real* to be a good actor.

David Dwight Eisenhower was graduated from Abilene High School in June, 1909. His scholastic record was not brilliant. True, he was in the upper third of his class, but the competition was not too stiff since there were only thirty-one boys and girls in it. In history, however, he was outstanding.

Ceil Curry drew the job of writing his pocket biography in the school annual, *The Helianthus*. She wrote that he "was interested in politics" and prophesied that "Ike will wind up as a professor of history at Yale."

Ceil's look into the future was not as far wrong as it seems at first glance. Ike never got to Yale, but he had a good deal to do with history.

The dog days hung heavily over Abilene in August, 1910. A blanket of heat that seemed suffocating and unending was spread over the land, and it took the heart out of a man. For the first time in his life—and almost the last—Ike was utterly discouraged. He had been out of school for over a year, and in all that time he felt that he had made no progress whatever.

Of course he had been very busy. He was night superintendent at the creamery. In addition, he did other odd jobs around town. He made minor repairs on the flashy automobiles trimmed with gleaming brass owned by a few well-to-do people north of the tracks.

All the extra money Ike made went to help Edgar through college. Arthur was helping Edgar, too, sending him five dollars a week out of his small earnings with the Commerce Trust Company.

Edgar, who graduated with Ike, wanted to be a lawyer. There was certainly not enough money for two Eisenhower boys to go to college at once.

"You know what you want to be, and I have no idea," Ike told his brother. "So it's only fair that you should have your chance. I'll stay out of school a year, anyhow, and send you what money I can."

The sacrifices that Ike and Arthur made were well rewarded by Edgar's accomplishments. In spite of having to earn most of his own way, he made a brilliant record in law school and is now one of the leading attorneys in Seattle, Washington.

Though he had no fixed ambition like his brother, Ike wanted more education. The longer he stayed out of school, the more he realized its necessity. Not that he begrudged Edgar his opportunity; he rejoiced in the reports of Edgar's rapid progress. But he felt within himself capabilities that might never be realized—certainly not at the creamery where the limit of ambition was the job of chief engineer held by his father.

Even smaller than the circle of business opportunity was the social round. Mostly it consisted of an occasional card game in the cellar of Joner Callahan's shop, or a small party at somebody's house, which Ike was generally too busy to attend. His greatest pleasure was going after rabbits and quail with the sixteen-gauge shotgun which he had extravagantly bought with eight hard-earned dollars.

So there were no far horizons for Ike. He seemed to be moving in a little circle. Looking forward, all he saw was himself coming around again.

In the back of Ike's mind there was one faint hope of escape. The seed of it had been planted there two months before. It flowered into determination in a casual conversation he had with Six MacDonell on an August afternoon. They were sitting idly on the curbstone in front of the Citizens Bank watching the buggies and heavily laden farm carts move slowly past in a golden shimmer of dust.

Ike spoke more casually than he felt. "Six,

let's you and me try to get into one of these service schools."

Six showed but the faintest interest. "What's that?"

"You know, Annapolis or West Point."

"What are they like?"

Ike's mind was vague about that. "I don't know," he admitted. "Only that from what Swede Hazlett says the life sounds pretty good. The government pays you while you learn—and play football!"

"Swede can go to Annapolis if he wants to," Six said. "Maybe he likes his looks all dressed up in a monkey suit with anchors on the collar. It wouldn't suit me!"

"That needn't bother us," Ike argued. "The main thing is that we'd get a chance to go to college."

"And play football for four more years!" put in Six.

"Sure," said Ike. "Come on, let's do it!"

"You do it," Six said. "Me, I'd rather play pro ball."

Ike had no illusions about his ability as a ballplayer. "I'm not that good. Besides, there's no future in it."

"No future," roared Six, snapping up straight. "Think of pitching a game for the Giants at the Polo Grounds in New York! What future is there in the Army?"

"I was thinking of the Navy," Ike said. He paused, and in that space made his decision. "I'm going to try for it."

Six only grunted.

"You don't have to stay in," Ike pointed out. "Unless there's a war."

"There won't be a war," Six said loudly. "The world's getting too civilized for war. It's silly to think about it."

"That makes it better," Ike answered. "I hate the idea of war."

CHAPTER 9

The Test in Topeka

Ike's decision to go to a service school was really the doing of Everett E. Hazlett—Swede as they called him. Hazlett, who was a year younger than Ike, had been at Abilene High with him for only one year, and then had gone to a military school in Wisconsin. He had always wanted to be an army officer, and pestered his congressman for an appointment to West Point. Finally, to get rid of him the congressman appointed Swede to the Naval Academy.

Hazlett accepted without much pleasure and hurried to a cramming school near Annapolis.

The time was too short for proper preparation and he failed in mathematics. But he had acquired a real enthusiasm for the Naval Academy and persuaded his much-bothered congressman to reappoint him for the following year.

Swede came back to Abilene determined to study like mad.

Ike was now night superintendent in full charge of the creamery from 6:00 P.M. to 6:00 A.M., and Swede often dropped by in the evening for a chat and a bit of food. One of the extras of Ike's job was permission to raid the cold storage room for ice cream and frozen chickens.

The two boys would scrub a coal shovel clean, then fry themselves a chicken over the banked fires under the boilers while they talked the night away. Swede's conversation was all about the wonders of Annapolis, and Ike caught fire from his enthusiasm.

"Why don't you try for it, too?" Swede urged. "We could have wonderful times there together."

"What chance have I got?" Ike asked. "You

already have the only appointment from this district."

"How about writing Senator Bristow?" Swede suggested. "He has appointments to give out."

"I might at that," Ike answered.

After his talk with Six MacDonell, Ike got busy. He went to call on Charles M. Harger of the *Reflector,* and his good friend Joseph W. Howe of the *News.* Both men were encouraging. Postmaster Phil Heath was not so optimistic. "Senator Bristow holds competitive examinations," he told Ike. "There will be about a hundred fellows after that appointment."

"Do you think I have a chance?" Ike asked.

Heath looked thoughtfully at the powerfully built young man who stood before him. He noted broad shoulders, the hard, compact body. Then he met the steady, serious blue eyes that looked straight into his own with intense determination.

"I reckon you're the sort of guy who can do just about anything you want to, if you hump yourself," he said.

In due course United States Senator Joseph L. Bristow of Kansas received a carefully written letter from David Dwight Eisenhower, stating his qualifications and asking to enter the competitive examinations for Annapolis. With it came enthusiastic recommendations from Ike's three older friends. Back came the senator's permission to compete in the examinations to be held at Topeka in October, 1910.

It was early September. That left only four weeks to make ready, and Ike had been out of school for a year!

It was then that Ike called out his full reserves of energy. He felt he must keep his night job at the creamery, but in the mornings he went back to high school to take special courses. For three hours every afternoon he went to the little office where Hazlett had a temporary job. Swede knew the ropes. He generously coached his friend in the requirements and short cuts he had learned in the cramming school at Annapolis.

On Saturday afternoons Ike played football. He cannot remember when he slept.

Swede Hazlett was amazed at the way his pupil's mind soaked up knowledge like a thirsty sponge. "In a few weeks Ike had outstripped me," he says.

In addition to his wonderfully retentive mind, Ike had one other advantage. During the year he thought of as wasted, he had spent much time in Joe Howe's office at the *News*. There he excitedly watched the telegraph instrument click out history as it was made throughout the world. And Mr. Howe had given him the run of his fine library. Thus Ike had never really stopped studying at all.

Going to Topeka was in itself quite an adventure for Ike. He had never had the time or money to go away from home. As the Union Pacific train steamed through the big brown fields and stopped at the little towns, he peered eagerly through the window, determined not to miss a thing.

Ike did not think he had much chance in the examinations. Young men from all over Kansas would be competing against him, and he was sure that some of them would be smarter than he.

But he did not let that upset him. He was determined to try his hardest. Worrying would not help—indeed, it would hurt his chances. It was part of his strength of character that once an issue was joined, he could put worry out of his mind.

Another characteristic of Ike's that helped him to become a great soldier was that he always weighed the situation calmly and then tried to arrange things so he got the best possible break. He figured that he might as well have two chances of getting an education as one, so he decided to take the examinations for both Annapolis *and* West Point. It was the luckiest decision he ever made.

It took several days to finish the two tests. Ike stayed at an inexpensive boardinghouse in

Topeka, and when he was not working in the crowded classrooms he made the most of his opportunity to see the little city, which seemed so big to his farm-bred eyes. Unlike most of the

other boys, he felt no sense of strain. So he had a wonderful time.

As he rode home again on the train he had no great hopes of victory. But he was at peace with himself, for he knew that he had done his best.

Swede Hazlett was sitting in his little office a few weeks later, boning up for Annapolis, when the door banged open and Ike charged in. One look at the broad grin on his face told the story.

"You won!" Swede exclaimed.

"I sure did!" Ike answered. "Look here! It says I made an average of 87.7 per cent in the Annapolis test. I was top man."

"By Jiminy that's great! Congratulations, Ike. What fun we'll have together!"

"We certainly will," Ike agreed. Then his face grew thoughtful. "But it means a lot more than fun to me, Swede. It means the chance to make something of myself. I began to think I'd never amount to shucks."

"With that brain of yours, you'd have gone to the top anyway," Swede argued loyally. "By the way, how did you come out in the West Point exam?"

"I got second," Ike answered indifferently. "But it doesn't matter, now."

YOUNG IKE

CHAPTER 10

Ike Joins the Army

True to the creed of the Brethren in Christ, Ida Eisenhower believed that fighting was a sin. She also had her own special reasons for hating war. When she was a little girl the Civil War was being fought. Her home stood in the path of battle that surged back and forth across Virginia. The armies of the North and the South fought in her front yard and all across the meadows where she liked to play. So she saw with her own frightened eyes the terror and brutality, the death and suffering, that war brought in its wake. No wonder she hated it!

When Ike told her he was going to try to become a naval officer she was very much troubled. But she did not beg him to give up the idea, or even let him see how unhappy she was. She believed that if you gave your children a good Christian upbringing you must trust them to do what was right.

If her son felt that he should go to the Naval Academy, it must be that God in his wisdom—and for some unknown purpose—willed it. So she accepted Ike's decision because she trusted him.

Meanwhile Ike was jubilant. For the next few weeks he continued to study hard in preparation for the actual entrance examinations to the Naval Academy. But there was no doubt in his mind that he could pass them. The way of his life seemed as straight as the railway line that ran through the Kansas prairies.

Then a crushing blow fell. He and Swede were reading over the requirements for the Naval Academy for the tenth time. Suddenly Swede said sharply, "Ike, how old will you be in June?"

"Twenty," Ike answered. "I was twenty on October 14."

"Gee! Gosh!" Swede groaned. "You're too old."

"What?" Ike demanded. "The age limits are sixteen to twenty."

"Yes, but look here! It says that means that you cannot have passed your twentieth birthday."

Ike grabbed the booklet. As he read it his high color drained away until his face looked like putty. "You're right," he said at last. "I guess I'm cooked."

"You needn't be," Swede said. "They don't demand a birth certificate. If you told them you were nineteen, nobody would ever know the difference."

"I'd know," Ike said gloomily. "I just couldn't do it."

The two boys sat slumped at the littered desk in utter misery.

"You should have tried for West Point," Swede said at last. "The age limits there are seventeen to twenty-one."

[79]

Ike came alive again. He was never the kind of man who gave up easily.

"Maybe I still can," he said. "I was second in the army test. Maybe the first guy will fail his physical or something. I'll write to Senator Bristow this minute."

That was perhaps the hardest letter he ever had to write, because it made him feel so foolish. He was sure the senator would be disgusted.

Another hard thing was to go to the men who had written the letters of recommendation for him and explain what had happened. They had been so proud of him when he won, and now he felt he had let them down.

But Charlie Harger and Joe Howe and Phil Heath stuck by him. They said that they were still proud of him—proud that he would admit his mistake. Proud of his integrity.

They all wrote again to Senator Bristow, who also valued honesty highly. He promised Ike the appointment if anything should happen to the boy who had won. When the latter failed his physical examination, the senator kept his word.

So, in the curious way of destiny, young Eisenhower was guided to the career in which he was able to serve his country supremely well.

On the afternoon Ike left for West Point most of the family were out. His father and Earl were at the creamery. Roy was working in the drugstore that summer—he later became a successful wholesale druggist. Only mother and Milton were at home. And, of course, Flip.

Flip was a fox terrier who had been in a dog act at the time the Parker Circus wintered in Abilene. One of the circus men had given the dog to Ike. Flip had given him complete canine devotion.

Flip was a very educated animal and he loved to do his tricks for Ike. He would come out of the hayloft window, high above the ground, run down the vertical side of the barn and jump straight out, landing on all four legs. He could also walk on his hind legs, jump through hoops and do very funny flip-flops.

It was going to be awfully hard to say good-by to Flip.

While Ike finished packing, his mother and Milton waited on the little side porch. It had never looked prettier, with red roses blooming on the trellis and the clear yellow light of afternoon making the grass seem very green. The freshness of early summer made the whole world look brand new.

At last they heard Ike's door slam, and the house shook as he ran downstairs. He came out on the porch and dropped his heavy suitcase with a crash.

"Are you sure you have everything you need?" Ida asked.

"Sure, Mother, I'll be all right. It will only be a couple of years till I see you."

"Oh, Dwight!" she whispered, and her tears flowed uncontrollably.

To Ike and Milton it was calamity—they had never seen their mother cry before.

Ike hugged Ida and kissed her hard.

Then he turned to his brother and in a queer,

rough voice said, "Milton, I'm depending on you to look after Mother."

It was more than Milton could bear. He began to bawl—loudly, childishly, as though his heart

were breaking. Flip joined in with a high-pitched, mournful howl.

"Stop it, please stop it," Ike begged, on the edge of tears himself. "Oh, for goodness sake!"

He grabbed his bag and ran down the street toward the station.

CHAPTER 11

Dedication

The most exciting part of Ike's trip to West Point
was the final stage. He boarded a special train at
Weehawken, New Jersey. The wooden day
coaches were full of boys. You could tell they
were nervous by the way they skylarked or sat
moodily silent. Ike was rather nervous, too, but
when he noticed how young most of the boys
looked, he felt better and tried to act a little
bored.

As the steam engine pulled the train out of the
station, it was difficult for Ike to keep up this
pretense. Across the wide, blue Hudson River

were the famous skyscrapers of New York. At their feet great, graceful ocean liners were loading for their voyages to all the distant seas.

In a few minutes New York was left behind. Tree-covered hills rolled down to the river. They seemed enormously high to Ike, who was used to the gently rolling prairies. And they kept getting higher. At last the train came to a place where the river narrowed to a sapphire ribbon of water over which dark and angry mountains crowded, shutting out the sky. Ike suddenly felt closed in and very homesick for the smiling Kansas plains.

The little wooden station at West Point was under a high cliff. Craning his neck to look at its top, Ike could see gray stone buildings that seemed to grow right out of the rock. One of them had a battlemented tower over which flew a big American flag.

The miscellaneous crowd of young men trudged up the hill in the hot sun carrying their bags. As they reached the top, Ike saw more turreted stone buildings half hidden by tall trees. To his right was an enormous level lawn. From the books he had read about West Point he knew that this was the parade ground. It was called "The Plain."

Soldiers were sitting at little wooden tables in front of the medieval portcullis of the Administration Building. The boys queued up in front of them to fill out the official forms. As Ike's turn came and he read the words in which he promised to serve in the Army of the United States for eight years from this day, he felt a sudden drag of doubt—this was an unalterable thing. For as he wrote his name, he would be signing away his freedom—his very life.

Then he snapped out of the dark mood. It was not as desperate as all that. It was only for eight years, he told himself. Casually he wrote "David Dwight Eisenhower"—almost the last time he ever signed his name that way.

For the first three weeks Ike and his classmates were called "beasts." The third classmen, who were given the job of breaking them in, were known as the "beast detail." Their methods of taming their supposedly wild charges were rough but effective.

Beasts had to do everything on the double— that is, at a dead run. That first day Ike ran to the barbershop to get his hair cropped. Then he ran to the cadet store for gray flannel trousers and a gray shirt; next, down to the basement for mattresses, pillows and gray army blankets; finally staggering under the load but still running, to his room in a stone barracks built around four sides of a court.

Next came a quick kindergarten sort of drill. Third classmen, looking very smart and shiny in razor-edged white duck trousers and beautifully fitted gray swallow-tailed coats trimmed with black braid and rows of gleaming brass buttons, herded the sweating beasts into an irregular line, then looked them over with disgust.

"You're the worst lot we ever had!"

"A disgrace to the Academy!"

Ike knew that just a year ago these very military young men had stood in just such a sloppy line. He grinned at the thought.

DEDICATION

"Hey, you big slob, what's your name?"

"Ike Eisenhower."

"Say sir to me, *Mister* Eisenhower. *And wipe off that smile!*"

Ike had a hard time obeying. This was a sort of game to him. He intended to keep the rules, but he had no intention of letting it get him down.

After what seemed like hours of stumbling around in the heat, the beasts were "marched" onto The Plain and formed up at one side. The sun was slanting down behind the hills, and long, cool shadows lay across the bright green turf. From the stone barracks came the swift beat of a lively march. Then, led by their band, the Corps of Cadets marched onto the field.

Ike had seen plenty of parades in Abilene on Decoration Day and the Fourth of July when veterans of the Civil War and volunteer firemen had marched up dusty Broadway. But he had never dreamed of anything like this.

[89]

Company after company in perfect lines swung across the parade ground. Hundreds of white-clad legs were moving in exact rhythm, gray-clad arms swinging all together, brass buttons flashing in the sun and the bright flags streaming out as the color guard went by.

Suddenly Ike found that he could no longer take it easy. The beauty and glory of the scene lifted his spirit to high emotion.

Then came the most solemn moment of all —when he and his new comrades took the oath of allegiance to their country. His voice grew husky as he repeated the sacred words:

"I do solemnly swear that I will support the Constitution of the United States and bear true allegiance to the National Government; that I will maintain and defend the sovereignty of the United States . . . and that I will at all times obey the legal orders of my superior officers and the rules and articles governing the Armies of the United States."

In that moment Ike dedicated himself forever to the service of his country.

CHAPTER 12

Code of Honor

Men are assigned to companies at West Point according to their height, so that on parade the line of heads going by is even. Ike's five feet ten and one-half inches rated Company F, the tallest on the left flank of the line. The men of Company F prided themselves on being the toughest in the corps. That suited Ike fine.

In the first weeks at the Academy, when friendships form which often last a lifetime, a man looks first among the members of his own company. Ike was lucky in finding among them two friends whose loyalty never wavered.

[91]

Very early he noticed a tall, thin boy who kept eying him shyly as they stood in the ranks. There was nothing shy about Ike. He decided he would like to know that boy and characteristically went straight up to him and said, "I'm Ike Eisenhower. What's your name?"

"Paul A. Hodgeson," was the reply. "I'm called P.A."

"Your accent sounds sort of familiar," Ike remarked. "Where are you from?"

"Wichita, Kansas."

Ike's face radiated pleasure. "I'm from Abilene! Want to be my tentmate at summer camp?"

"You bet," said P.A.

After that P.A. and Ike roomed together throughout their whole four years at the Academy. In West Point slang they were "wives."

P.A. turned out to be a crack athlete. He won his *A* in football, played baseball, basketball and was good at track, where he broke the record for the high jump and the broad jump.

Better still, he was a fine scholar and extremely conscientious. P.A. used to worry a great deal about Ike's careless attitude toward the rules. "Mister" Eisenhower was often in hot water, and it was due to P.A.'s fussing that he did not get into more trouble.

Ike's next best friend was a lanky cadet from Moberly, Missouri, who did not join Company F until the following year. He was a brilliant pitcher on the Army team and could make a baseball do nip ups between the mound and the plate. He was not the least bit good looking. In fact, with his long face, full lips, lank hair and small brown eyes he looked a little like a monkey. But everyone who knew him liked him immensely, and his friendship with Ike grew stronger throughout the long years. His name was Omar Bradley and he became Ike's most trusted general in the great campaign for the liberation of Europe.

They number the classes backward at West Point and Annapolis. That is, a senior is a first classman, while the Fourth Class is the lowest. Fourth classmen are called plebes.

[93]

A plebe is the lowest form of life at the Academy. He has to say "sir" to all his "elders," and follow a group of traditional rules which include never speaking to an upperclassman unless spoken to; sitting upright on the edge of his chair at meals; receiving a lot of hazing, which was sometimes pretty rough in Ike's day, and taking orders from everybody. There is a ritual which every plebe must learn and which Ike observed many times. It consists of a series of questions put by an upperclassman to which the answers are always the same. In them the plebe describes himself as lowly, humble and completely unworthy.

The final question is, "Whom does a plebe rank?" (i.e., who is he above). The answer is, "The superintendent's dog, the commandant's cat and all the admirals in the whole darn Navy."

Ike didn't mind the hazing much. He took it casually as part of the game. But he was as impudent as he dared to be. There was the famous occasion on which some upperclassmen ordered that "Cadets Eisenhower and Larkin will appear at our rooms in full-dress coats immediately after taps."

"It's an order," Ike said. "We'll obey it exactly."

As the last mournful note of the final bugle call died away, Mr. Eisenhower and Mr. Larkin presented themselves to their seniors. Those gentlemen gaped at the most extraordinary spectacle they had ever seen.

The military splendor of full-dress coats with their gleaming buttons and white crossbelts was made more dazzling by the fact that the two cadets wore absolutely nothing from the waist down.

One upperclassman tried to roar in his rage and only succeeded in croaking out, "What's the meaning of this?"

Very respectfully Cadet Eisenhower answered, "Nothing was said about trousers, sir."

Though Ike often broke the rules, he always was true to the West Point code of honor. This is terrifically strict by civilian standards. Each cadet is placed on his honor never to lie or cheat in any way, and never under any circumstances to break his word. It is all right to break the rules if someone else is responsible for seeing that you keep them. If you are in charge of a section, how-

ever, you must even report yourself if you do wrong.

All of the cadet's misdeeds are recorded in a little book called the "skin sheets." Each offense rates a certain number of demerits, and the punishment is usually so many hours of marching all by yourself in the "Area," carrying a heavy rifle.

Ike did a good deal of this solitary marching, for he received a lot of demerits. You can find them still, written in the faded pages of the old "skin sheets":

Demerits

Not standing steady in ranks 3

Wearing very dirty white trousers. About 9:00 A. M. 2

Improper expression. About 2:35 P. M. . . . 4

Asleep in chair at inspection, 8:30 P. M. . . . 2

Trifling with the corporal of the guard after supper 4

Hanging head and gazing at ground while marching to breakfast 2

Each of these "skins" is signed by the officer or cadet who reported it. Then comes one which shows how completely Ike respected the honor code.

Not staying in area between tattoo and taps as directed

(signed) *Eisenhower*

This carried the heavy penalty of five demerits and meant weary hours of marching.

West Point did not teach Ike not to lie and cheat—his mother's upbringing did that. But it did strengthen his moral sense to the point where the slightest slip from its strict code was unthinkable to him.

The West Point motto is: "Duty. Honor. Country." All his life Eisenhower has lived up to that code.

CHAPTER 13

Brief Glory

The people of the United States first heard the name of Eisenhower when Ike was a third classman—a yearling—at the Military Academy. It was his first and—for many long, long years—his only touch of glory.

In the fall of 1912 Ike became a star halfback on the Army team. In his plebe year he had played brilliantly on the Cullum Hall Squad, which corresponds to the freshman team at college. Now he made the varsity, the big gold *A*. There was nothing casual about the way Ike played football. He put his heart and soul into it, playing with all the courage and intense determination that in later years was to make him a great leader of men.

In the very first game of the season Ike made his mark. He was the second-string left halfback, but Geoffrey Keyes, the first-string man, was injured in a practice scrimmage, so Ike ran onto the field with the Army team. Tackling hard, blocking beautifully and charging through the line with the tremendous power of one hundred and ninety pounds of bone and spring steel muscle, he contributed heavily to Army's 27-0 victory over Stevens.

The following week Keyes was still laid up, and Ike again starred as Army beat Rutgers 19-0.

Now the sports writers began to open their eyes. Under a two-column picture of Ike punting, the New York *Times* called him "one of the most promising backs in Eastern football." Other papers sang his praises. They called him "The huge Kansan." His teammate P.A., who was even bigger, was referred to by the picturesque press as "The gigantic Kansan."

[100]

Unluckily, Eisenhower's varsity football career was as brilliant and brief as one of those bright shooting stars that flash across the velvet summer sky. Its end came six weeks after it began.

On November 9, 1912, the Carlisle Indians played West Point. It was a massacre—the redskins did everything but scalp Army. Jim Thorpe, a young Indian who was perhaps the greatest all-round athlete America ever produced, was the star of the Carlisle team. That day the Army couldn't stop him. He slipped through the line like a well-oiled eel for huge gains, or ran around end with such flashing speed that the Army tacklers looked as though they were growing like trees. Ike tells how he and P.A. tried to stop Thorpe.

"I think he's coming through the line this play," Ike said. "If he does, you hit him high and I'll hit his legs. That ought to fix him."

As Ike had foreseen, Thorpe did come through the line, and was hit according to plan. They stopped the Indian that time, and left him lying breathless on the turf. But on the very next play, Jim Thorpe hit the line again, going through for ten yards!

It was a clean game but a very rough one. The final score was Carlisle 27-Army 6. Worse by far than the defeat was the fact that Ike had wrenched his knee.

Marty Mahr, the tough little trainer of the Army team, worked feverishly all week to get Ike's knee back in condition. He even ordered a special brace, designed to hold it steady in the rough-and-tumble of the scrimmage. Ike was wearing it on the following Saturday as he trotted out on the field in his black and gold uniform for the game against Tufts College.

If the Carlisle game had been a massacre, the game against Tufts was Ike's personal Waterloo. Midway through it his weakened knee collapsed with badly torn ligaments. Stretcher bearers trotted out. As Ike was lifted up and carried from the field, he turned his head to see the gray-clad ranks of cadets standing in their section of the wooden bleachers. For the last time he heard the thrilling cheer:

sssSSS . . . . BOOM . . . . Ahhh
U.S.M.A. Rah! Rah!
Hoo-rah! Hoo-rah.
Ar MAY! Rah!
Eisenhower! Eisenhower! Eisenhower!

Chief Surgeon Charles Keller was a fine doctor and a kind man. The cadets loved him. A little song they used to sing about him showed this:

We will send you down to Doctor Keller
He will make you sick or weller
He will part you from your inmost thoughts.

Dr. Keller took great care of Ike.

"Do you think I'll be able to play in the Navy game?" Ike asked, gritting his teeth against the pain.

"No!" Dr. Keller told him sadly. "You will have to lie flat on your back for a month."

It was a terrible disappointment to Ike, for the Navy game is the only game that really *counts* with the cadets.

But when the first black despair passed, Ike took a philosophical attitude. He studied extra hard to keep up with his classes. P.A. and his other friends came to cheer him up, and he had time to do a good deal of outside reading. Mostly, he concentrated on getting well. For Dr. Keller was hopeful that his knee would heal completely.

But something happened that kept Ike from ever playing against Navy.

By January Dr. Keller pronounced Ike fit for limited service. "Favor your knee," he ordered. "And don't do anything strenuous."

"How about the drills?" Ike asked.

"You'll be all right except for riding drill. You must *not* mount and remount."

"Yes, sir," Ike said.

Dr. Keller clapped him affectionately on the shoulder. "Take it easy and you'll play Navy yet."

Ike followed his orders carefully and got along very well. His knee was becoming better every day. The marching did not bother him at all, and at riding class he just stayed on his horse, for mounting and dismounting was a terrible strain on his bad knee.

However, this did not suit the riding instructor at all. He scowled and made unpleasant remarks. Each day he seemed to get more irate, for one lone cadet remaining on horseback when the others dismounted spoiled the symmetry of the drill. Finally he became absolutely furious.

"Mr. Eisenhower!" he shouted. "You're faking. I order you to dismount and mount with the class."

Ike's face went white. His blue eyes got as bleak as a Kansas blizzard. This was petty tyranny in the guise of discipline. He could have refused to obey, and Dr. Keller would have backed him up. But the riding master's spiteful accusation of faking seemed to touch his honor. He was so infuriated that for once he lost his head.

"Yes, sir," he said sullenly.

Was it twelve times or twenty that Ike dismounted and remounted his horse during that long drill? He never could remember. All he knew was that each time his knee grew worse, until toward the end the searing agony made him sway in the saddle on the verge of fainting.

Somehow, on sheer nerve, he went through it

to the bitter end. He dismounted from his horse for the last time, walked a few stumbling steps and collapsed in the tanbark of the ring.

Dr. Keller was so angry that his waxed mustache seemed to crackle electrically; he was so mad he almost cried.

"You young fool," he sputtered. "Why did you do it? Why?"

"He said I was faking," Ike answered through clenched teeth. "I had to show him I wasn't yellow."

"I'd like to whip him with his own riding crop!" Keller growled. "And you, too, for your silly pride."

"Will it ever get well?" Ike asked faintly.

"I don't know," Keller said. "Certainly you'll never play football again. You may not even be fit to graduate."

Actually, Ike's knee never got completely well. It is still a little wonky even today, and once, when he was supreme commander in Europe, he strained it badly and had to have it bandaged up stiff. But he did not let it interfere with his duties. He even continued his regular visits to the troops at the front, although the bouncing jeep he rode in caused him acute pain.

Had it not been for Dr. Keller he would not have been able to get his commission. The surgeon cared for him with great skill and tenderness, and when the time came for Ike's final physical examination Dr. Keller, knowing by then that the knee would probably continue to improve, stretched a point and pronounced him fit for active service.

CHAPTER 14

Abilene Again

Two years is a long time to be away from home. It seemed especially long to Ike as he traveled westward on his month's leave that summer of 1913. So many things had happened that Abilene and the small white house and even his family were like distant memories.

The train arrived late in the evening, and as Ike stepped off at the once familiar station his feeling of strangeness increased. There was no one to meet him, so he picked up his bag and walked alone along the dark street, seeing it as though for the first time.

He cut across the vacant lot, looking at the shadowy outline of his home against the stars. The windows were dark; they had all gone to bed.

Ike was suddenly very lonely. This was not the way he had pictured it during those long, long years. Then he heard a sharp, inquiring bark and answered with one clear whistle.

There was a streak of white that took off across the field. He dropped his bag and caught the flying bundle of dog like a forward pass. Then Flip was wriggling in his arms, whining with excitement and violently licking his face.

It was wonderful to be home, wonderful to see Dad and Mother and Milton again. The first thing Ike did after greeting them was to run all over the house to make sure nothing was changed. All his life he did that when he came back from the far-off places to which the Army sent him. He wanted his home to be just as he remembered it as a boy.

ABILENE AGAIN

It was fun getting to know Abilene again. It looked smaller than he remembered it, but he loved it dearly. And he liked catching up with all his old friends—Paul Royer, the Sterls and Six MacDonell, who was playing professional baseball now.

When Ike went calling on the girls they treated him with a great deal more respect, now that he was a West Pointer. On leave he wore civies, but Ceil Curry got him to put on his full-dress uniform for their benefit. They ohed and ahed when they saw him—and not without reason. His high color, bright blue eyes, short yellow hair and strong body shown off by the beautifully fitted uniform made him a handsome figure of a young man. Ike was embarrassed to the point of blushing by their admiration, but he was mighty pleased by it, too.

His best girl that summer was Gladys Harding, a radiantly blond young lady with a lovely soprano voice. She had signed up with a traveling concert company to sing and play the piano, and was going on tour in the fall.

Ike was fascinated by her talent and beauty, while she enjoyed his gay companionship.

"I have more fun with you than any man I ever knew," she told him.

They thought they were in love and made great plans to meet when she should come east on her tour. They did meet once when Ike got Christmas leave and took her dancing in New York. But they were not really in love. Gladys continued her career and Ike was too busy in his last year at the Point to think about girls at all.

During his short summer leave in Abilene Ike had only one real adventure. It was one he did not seek; he was shoved into it.

While he had been away Abilene had developed a boxing champion. Dirk Tyler was a young Negro who had made quite a name for himself, first as an amateur and then as a professional fighter. He had easily licked all the boys in town, and when Ike's friends heard that he had done quite a bit of boxing at West Point, they plagued him to fight Tyler.

"I don't see any point in it," Ike said. "I'm on vacation and all I want to do is to take it easy."

One day Ike was having his hair cut in the barbershop where Tyler worked as a porter. Bill Sterl came in to get a shave, but promptly forgot about that.

"When are you two going to fight for the championship of Abilene?" he asked.

Dirk Tyler grinned amicably. "I'll take Ike on any time he likes," he said confidently.

Ike did not like it one bit. His knee was still stiff and weak, while Tyler looked perfectly enormous. But the honor of West Point seemed somehow at stake.

"I'll fight him right now," Ike said.

"Great," Bill Sterl said excitedly. "We'll put the match on in Father's gym."

The "Champ's Gym" was in the basement of Sterl's Department Store. Everybody moved across the street to it, including the barber and a half-shaved customer. Mr. Sterl himself came down to referee, followed by all his clerks. Business stopped dead in Abilene as the word of the fight spread, and shopkeepers and customers crowded into the camp chairs around the ring in Sterl's basement.

When Dirk Tyler took off his shirt, Ike liked the look of things still less. The muscles under his opponent's dark shining skin bulged like bunches of oranges. Dirk was taller than he and a good twenty pounds heavier. Ike could picture what would happen if one of those great fists collided with his nose. Telling about that fight, he says frankly, "I was scared stiff."

Mr. Sterl saw that their gloves were on right and gave them some very professional-sounding instructions about the rules: "No hitting below the belt. Go to your corners when a round is over."

Then he pulled out his fat, old-fashioned silver watch, studied it for a moment, then in a voice that sounded to Ike like the clap of doom he called, "TIME!"

The two boys came out of their corners, touched gloves and dropped into a fighting pose.

[114]

Then Ike's face broke into a wide grin of sheer relief.

Dirk Tyler had assumed an awkward position with his arms crossed in front of him. Ike had learned a lot about the art of boxing at the Point, and he saw that Dirk had only sheer power without the skill to use it.

Ike began dancing around. His knee in its elastic stocking felt fine now. Dirk threw a terrific punch that went by with a whoosh as Ike ducked. Tyler swung again and Ike blocked with his left. They fought so for a few moments, Ike dancing away, Dirk lunging at him with tremendous blows. If just one of them had hit, Ike would have been knocked flat.

Then Ike saw the opening he had been waiting for. He stepped forward on his good leg, and brought his left fist up against his opponent's chin. Dirk's head came up with the blow and Ike let go his right. That ended the fight. It had lasted less than three minutes.

They carried Dirk back to the barbershop feet first. Ike helped to revive him with witch hazel from the barber's supply. There were no hard feelings.

When Dirk came to, he grinned sheepishly and said, "You won!"

"I was lucky," Ike said.

Although this was not quite true, he wanted to make Dirk feel better.

After that the two young men became great friends.

The thirty days of Ike's leave whizzed by awfully fast. When the moment came to say goodby, he felt even sadder than the first time he left. The two years ahead of him seemed to stretch lonely and endless.

Yet when he reached the Academy it was not so bad. He was glad to see his friends again. They all had a great deal to say to each other. Even the gray stone buildings and the beautiful green expanse of The Plain had a pleasantly familiar look. The fact is that West Point had become a second home to Ike.

CHAPTER 15

The Last Parade

During Ike's last year at West Point he was forced to take his career very seriously. He had gone to the Military Academy mainly to get an education. The idea of being a soldier did not especially appeal to him. In that time of profound peace the whole business of uniforms, drills and preparing for war seemed a little like play acting.

In the summer of 1914, however, this serene sense of safety was blown to bits by the opening cannonade of World War I. As Ike read the terrible news from Europe of bloody battles, of devastated cities and ruined farms, he realized that if old civilized countries like France and England and Germany could be stricken by the horrors of war, even America was not safe. Suddenly he knew that he might have to fight in defense of his country.

That made the training at West Point very real indeed. He decided that it was his duty to make himself the best possible sort of soldier. As a result, he no longer treated the drills and disciplines with carefree tolerance. He went seriously to work to fit himself for a military career.

In his spare time he often went to the Battle Monument at the end of The Plain and sat thinking about the history of the United States. In the days of the American Revolution this very spot had been the most important fort for the defense of America. The funny old cannon that pointed down at the narrow stretch of river had kept the British ships from sailing up to Albany and cutting the American colonies in two. At Ike's feet were foot-long links of the great iron chain which had been stretched across the Hudson to keep those ships from slipping by at night.

The thought of the patriots who had fought

against such terrible odds to win freedom for their country strengthened Eisenhower's determination to fit himself to help defend her hard-won liberty. He knew that playtime was over.

June, 1915, came at last. Four years ago in Abilene it had looked very far away. Looking backward, those years seemed to have shortened like a closed-up telescope.

So Ike came to his final dress parade. He was color sergeant of the corps, and as he marched in those perfect ranks across The Plain for the last time, the Stars and Stripes floated over his head from its polished staff.

Straight as though measured by an enormous ruler, the long gray lines stood at present arms. Fixed bayonets shone like motionless flames in the slanting sunshine; the drawn swords of the cadet officers were as steady as though the men holding them were cast in bronze. Ike stood as rigid as the rest. Only the flag stirred gently in the evening breeze.

[119]

With a splendid crash of harmony the b
burst into the National Anthem. As the sole
notes rose and fell, the statuelike figure of
young color sergeant was swept by wild tides
emotion. His mouth was dry, his lips set in a gri.
military mask; but his heart was pounding i.
triple rhythm. The sweet final notes were almos
more than he could bear:

> *. . . long may it wave*
> *O'er the land of the free and the home of the*
>   *brave!*

As the last note echoed back from the rocky
hills of the Hudson Valley, a cannon barked
once. The thin veil of smoke from its muzzle
drifted back across those rigid lines. For a few
moments that seemed like an eternity, there was
absolute stillness on The Plain. No one moved,
no one spoke. It was the silence of dedication.

Once Ike had thought that when he received
his diploma and the golden bars were pinned

upon his shoulder straps it would be the end of his bondage. Now he knew it was only the beginning. Henceforward, to whatever station he was called, Dwight D. Eisenhower would devote his whole life to the service of his country.

CHAPTER 16

Supreme Commander

After a short leave in Abilene, Second Lieutenant Dwight D. Eisenhower was ordered to join the Nineteenth Infantry at Fort Sam Houston at San Antonio, Texas. So he came back at last to his native state. Good things always happened to Ike in Texas. It was there that he met Mamie Dowd.

Mamie was a very pretty girl with masses of soft brown hair, blue eyes that shone with a special brilliance and an exquisitely fair skin. Though she looked fragile, she was a good sport with a wonderful sense of humor.

She was out for a Sunday afternoon drive with her father and mother when they decided to stop by Fort Sam for supper with some friends. There were several young officers present, among them a big young man with thin yellow hair and a round smiling face. He had the bluest, merriest eyes Mamie had ever seen.

After supper Ike Eisenhower said, "Would you like me to show you around the post, Miss Dowd?"

"I'd love it," Mamie said enthusiastically, although she had seen Fort Sam many times.

On that walk around the fort they discovered how much they liked each other and how much fun they had together.

The next day Mamie went fishing at a near-by lake. When she got home the maid said, "Miss Mamie, there's been a Lieutenant Eisenhart calling you every fifteen minutes all day long."

"You must mean Eisenhower," Mamie said. "I wonder if he'll call again."

Just then the telephone rang.

That was the beginning of Ike's strenuous courtship. Mamie Dowd had lots of other beaux,

[124]

but they did not have a chance against the eager young lieutenant.

Mamie and Ike became engaged on St. Valentine's Day, 1916, and they were married at the Dowds' summer home in Denver, Colorado, on July 1. Like the people in the old fairy tales they lived happily ever after.

Soon after Ike's marriage, in April, 1917, Germany's ruthless sinking of American ships forced the United States to enter World War I on the side of England and France and all the Allies. Much to his disgust, Lieutenant Eisenhower did not see action in this war. But what he did do proved to be even better training for his future responsibilities.

On March 1, 1918, Eisenhower, who had been promoted to captain, was ordered to command the Tank Training Center at Camp Colt, Gettysburg, Pennsylvania. It was an unusually important post for a young captain. Ike had twenty thousand men to be trained in tank warfare, but because every machine the Allies had was needed for the great battles in France, he was only given one small tank with which they could practice. Despite this, Ike worked out such a good train-

ing program that the men he sent to France were almost ready for front-line service.

When the war ended in the defeat of Germany on November 11, 1918, Eisenhower, who had become a temporary lieutenant colonel, was sent to Camp Meade, Pennsylvania. Almost the first person he met there was a tall, thin officer whose polished boots flashed like mirrors in the sun and who wore a chestful of battle ribbons. It was Colonel George S. Patton, Jr., who had commanded the American Tank Brigade in France.

"You're the guy who trained my boys," Patton exclaimed, giving him a hearty handshake.

"And you commanded them in battle," Ike said enviously. "Were they good?"

"The best," said Patton. "You did a swell job."

The two young officers soon became great friends. They were both convinced of the importance of tanks in future warfare. "We'll use them as they did the knights in armor in the old days," Patton exclaimed. "That's what they'll be, the armored cavalry of the future!"

Patton and Eisenhower met almost every evening to study and plan. Together they worked out the tactics which they used with such brilliant success in World War II.

For a little while after World War I, it seemed as though permanent peace had come at last. The peoples of the world were sickened by the horrors of modern war. Almost all the countries banded together in the League of Nations designed to prevent war, and the United States took the lead in a series of conferences at which the great powers agreed to reduce the size of their armies and navies. Like most Americans, Eisenhower hoped and believed that there would not be another war—at least not for a very long time.

In 1921 Ike was ordered to Camp Gaillard in the Panama Canal Zone to help General Fox Connor plan new defenses for the canal which was so vital to the safety of America. Panama was the first of the many strange, far places in which Mamie made a home for Ike.

This one was in a funny old house that stood on stilts on a hillside by the canal. It had porches all around, and the windows had no glass because it is always hot in tropical Panama.

It was a very nice house except for the bats—there were hundreds of those flying mouselike

[128]

creatures. Mamie was a very brave young woman, but she was scared of bats.

One night after Ike and Mamie had gone to bed, a bat got into their room. As it zoomed around, Mamie hid her head under the bedclothes. "Kill it, Ike!" she begged. "Please do something."

Ike jumped out of bed and grabbed a cavalry saber. He must have looked very funny indeed as he chased that bat around the room in his pajamas, swinging the great, curved sword. Up over the bed Ike went. He jumped on chairs and tables, while the "enemy" maneuvered like a jet plane. Finally he made a tremendous lunge that hit the mark.

"You can come out now, Mamie," he said. "The infantry just won over air power."

Two very important things happened to Ike while he was in Panama. The first was the birth of his son John Dowd Eisenhower, who grew up to follow in his father's footsteps as an army officer. The second concerned a talk Ike had with his commanding officer.

General Fox Connor was a wise and thoughtful man. Unlike most people, he saw that World War I had settled nothing. "America is in deadly peril," he told Eisenhower one night. "In the last war we fought for an ideal and the right to live in peace; the next time we will be fighting for our very lives."

"When do you think it will come?" Ike asked.

"Maybe ten, maybe twenty years," said General Connor. "I shall be too old. It will be up to men like you. For years America will go on unheeding, then she will cry for help in panic and distress. Make yourself ready to answer when she calls!"

So Ike dedicated himself anew to the service of his country.

The first step was to go to the General Staff School at Fort Leavenworth, Kansas. It was far tougher than West Point, for Ike was competing against the best brains in the whole Army. He was graduated first in his class.

The remaining years of peace were a period of intense training and education for Ike. He was sent to France where he studied the battlefields of World War I, and the geography of the country where he might someday have to fight again. Then he became an aide to General MacArthur, who was chief of staff in Washington, under whom he learned the ways of the high command.

When MacArthur went to the Philippines to teach the people of the Islands how to build an army for their defense against Japan, he took Eisenhower with him. Together they trained the Philippine Army and worked out the plans for the defense of Bataan which MacArthur carried out so heroically when Japan attacked.

At Baguio in the wooded Philippine Hills, Ike learned to pilot a plane. One time he was nearly killed when the controls of his plane got jammed. But he kept his head and succeeded in fighting the plane down to a safe landing.

Learning to fly was another step in the education of Eisenhower, for he learned to understand the problems of airmen.

Ike was still in the Philippines when Germany, having grown strong again under the ruthless leadership of Adolf Hitler, once more attacked her European neighbors. This was the war Fox Connor had foreseen. Ike asked for transfer home.

While Germany conquered France, battered Britain with her terrible bombers and attacked Russia, Eisenhower helped to train the troops needed to defend America.

In October, 1941, Ike was promoted to brigadier general. There was a parade in his honor, and he took his first salute as a general at Fort Sam Houston to which he had gone as a newly fledged second lieutenant.

On December 7, 1941, Japan treacherously bombed our fleet at Pearl Harbor. Germany declared war on us. Attacked from two sides, America was fighting for her life.

In the first days of World War II, General George C. Marshall ordered Brigadier General Eisenhower to Washington in charge of war plans. As America grew stronger and troops were sent to England, Lieutenant General Eisenhower was placed in command of them.

Then in November, 1942, came the first great

Allied effort of the war, the attempt to free North Africa from German control. Eisenhower was appointed to command the British and American forces. From his headquarters on the Rock of Gibraltar he watched the great fleet of warships and transports sail by, carrying a hundred thousand men who would gain victory or taste bitter defeat—depending on how well he commanded them.

Everyone has read of the long, hard fight for Africa and the victory finally won. The freeing of Sicily followed. Then in September, 1943, American and British troops under Eisenhower landed in Italy on the mainland of Europe.

Eisenhower won these first battles of the war by the excellence of his judgment and his ability to inspire the troops under his command to great deeds. His leadership had joined England and America into one great winning team.

For these reasons President Franklin D. Roosevelt and Prime Minister Winston Churchill of England, with the advice of their generals, appointed Eisenhower supreme commander of the great armies that were gathering in England to free Europe from the evil rule of Hitler's Nazi Germany.

Hitler had made Europe into a fortress—ringed with guns. Its beaches were covered with barbed wire and defended by the mighty German Army. To attack it seemed a desperate venture, and many military men thought it would end in disaster.

Eisenhower made his plans carefully with the aid of many brilliant soldiers. Chief among them was British Air Marshal A. W. Tedder, General Bernard Montgomery and Ike's great friend and classmate General Omar Bradley. In addition, thousands of American and British officers worked night and day on the very complicated plans.

The day set for the invasion was called D day. The date was June 6, 1944. It was kept very secret so the Germans would not know about it in advance.

The morning before D day was very stormy,

but since the weathermen said it would clear up next day, at 3:00 A.M. Eisenhower, who was a five-star general now, gave the order that started thousands of ships plunging through the great waves toward Normandy in France.

Ike spent the day seeing the troops off. Last of all he went to one of the fields from which the paratroopers were taking off for the most dangerous mission of all—to drop behind the enemy lines.

Those men whom he was sending into such awful danger cheered him wildly. He shook hands with as many as possible. Then he went to the observation tower to watch the tow planes haul the gliders into the evening sky. As the great aerial fleet formed into squadrons and headed for France, Ike took off his cap and prayed: "God keep them safe."

The plans had been well made. In landing craft and small boats, American and British stormed ashore, while warships bombarded the forts and airplanes guarded the sky and bombed the enemy.

On June 7 Ike boarded a British cruiser and sailed down the white-capped English Channel to see how the fight was going. General Montgomery came aboard to report to the supreme commander. "Your Americans were magnificent," he said, "and so were my Northumbrians."

As the little Britisher climbed back down the ladder to his boat, Ike leaned over the rail and called, "Good luck to you!"

On the sixth day of the landing, Ike went ashore on the beach near Isigny to talk with the troops who had fought so bravely.

The Germans fought hard and well. For over a month they kept the Allies penned up in Normandy. Ike had expected that. He planned a great battle in which the Americans broke through the German lines. Then he sent his old friend Georgie Patton out with Third Army. Just as they had planned long ago, Patton swept through France with his tanks. In a few short weeks the German armies were driven back to their own country. France was free again.

There was still a lot of hard fighting to be done. Europe would not be safe for free men until the Nazis were beaten. The war lasted all through the winter. Though Ike had to be at headquarters a good deal to plan the battles, he spent all his free time visiting the troops. In jeeps and little planes he went to all the front lines. Everywhere the soldiers were glad to see him and cheered madly. They affectionately called him "General Ike."

At last, in the spring, with the help of the big Russian armies and the brave French, Germany was invaded and defeated. Adolf Hitler was dead and the Nazi generals asked for peace.

Ike's headquarters were in a red brick school-house at Rheims in France. In a big classroom with blackboards and maps around the walls, the Nazi generals signed the paper that surrendered to the Allies.

Peace was won at last.

CHAPTER 17

President Ike

When the war ended Ike was the hero of the whole free world. Probably never before in history had a man been so beloved and admired by people of so many nations. Wherever he went— in Paris, London, Washington and New York— enormous crowds turned out shouting affectionately, "Ike! Ike!"

The greatest day of all was when he came home to Abilene in a long special train. Mamie was with him. His brothers and old friends were there, and thousands of people from the whole countryside came to greet him. Ida Eisenhower sat proudly beside her son on the reviewing stand to watch the parade in his honor.

Then all the Eisenhowers went home to the little white house on Fourth Street, which had not been changed a bit.

From the moment when Germany surrendered, Ike decided that he would devote the rest of his life to peace. He resolved to do everything possible so that men would never again have to live through the horror and misery of war.

His first task was to teach Germany to govern itself as a democracy, and to help the German people rebuild their ruined cities.

When he got this well started, the President sent for him to become Chief of Staff of the United States Army. This was another big job. Ike had to let as many of the soldiers as possible go home, yet still keep the Army strong enough to guard America.

Eisenhower spent over two years in Washington as Chief of Staff. Then feeling that his work was done, he asked the President to relieve him of active duty.

Columbia University in New York asked him to become its president. Ike accepted because, as he said, "I want to be with young people—to help them to find the road to peace."

Ike was made president of Columbia at a solemn ceremony in the great court of the university in October, 1948. Scholars came from all over the world to honor him. When he had received the "golden key" of office and made a moving speech, he left the platform. Ahead of him marched the mace bearer, and following two by two came the presidents of universities and famous scholars wearing their black gowns with hoods of many bright colors. As Eisenhower reached the botton step ten thousand people stood in silent salute to him.

Ike paced slowly along until he came to the spot where Mamie was standing in the front row of the crowd. Then he did a very unmilitary thing. He stepped out of line—and the whole parade stopped in confusion. Ike ran to Mamie and whispered something to her. Then he skipped quickly back into line and solemnly marched ahead.

What he had said to his dear wife was, "Don't you ever stand up because of me, Mamie!"

During the two years he was president of Columbia, Eisenhower did many things to further the cause of peace. But he was not allowed to finish his work there.

Once again the peace of the world was in danger. War had broken out in Korea. The Communists in Russia had raised great armies that threatened to invade Europe. The President sent for Ike and asked him to go to France to organize the free nations of Europe to defend themselves. He was, the President said, the only man whom the European people trusted to do the job.

In January, 1951, Ike and Mamie sailed for France. There Ike worked with Frenchmen, Britains, Italians, Norwegians, Belgians, Dutch, with his former enemies the Germans and, of course, with many Americans, welding them into a team to defend the free world.

Meanwhile, more and more people in America wanted Ike to come home and be their president. They felt that the country needed his inspiring leadership. Politicians began to come to SHAPE, as Ike's headquarters in the French forest of Marly was called, to ask him if he would accept the Republican nomination for president in 1952.

Ike had no political ambitions. But he was very conscious of the dangerous state of the world. And he *was* ambitious to preserve peace. In the end he yielded to this call to further serv-

[143]

ice—in his heart he had known all along that he would.

When Ike said good-by to his associates at SHAPE those hard-shelled military men of many nations were visibly touched. As the supreme commander turned to leave the great hall where the final meeting was held, Field Marshal Montgomery sprang forward to shake his old comrade's hand. "God bless you, Ike!" he said.

At the Republican Convention in Chicago they nominated Dwight D. Eisenhower as their candidate for President of the United States. Then Ike and Mamie stood on the platform together while the hall rocked to

the wild cheering of more than a thousand delegates.

It was a hard-fought campaign. Ike traveled by train and plane all over America, speaking to millions of his fellow countrymen, telling them what he would do if he were elected.

On Election Day, 1952, the American people unmistakably voiced their faith in the leadership of Ike Eisenhower. By thirty-three million votes, the greatest number ever cast for a candidate, he was elected President of the United States.

At his campaign headquarters in the Hotel Commodore in New York, Ike received the news of his great victory with humble gratitude. He knew that the hardest job of all lay ahead.

As he came into the brilliant ballroom of the hotel—with Mamie beside him—he was greeted by a typhoon of cheering from his jubilant supporters. But when he spoke to them his voice was solemn, almost sad, as though the great task he had undertaken weighed upon his spirit. After thanking them and the American people for their confidence he turned, as he always has, to bringing people to work together for the good of all.

"Let us unite for the better future of America," he said, "for our children and our grandchildren. We cannot do the job ahead of us except as a united people."